Contemporary Stained Glass Sidelights

Jody Wright

DOVER PUBLICATIONS, INC.
Mineola, New York

Bibliographical Note

Contemporary Stained Glass Sidelights, first published by Dover Publications, Inc., in 2006, contains all of the designs from *20 Floral Sidelights, 20 Nature Sidelights,* and *20 Geometric Sidelights* by Jody Wright, originally published by WSG Publications, Martinsburg, West Virginia, in 2003.

DOVER *Pictorial Archive* SERIES

International Standard Book Number: 0-486-45367-7

Manufactured in the United States of America
Dover Publications, Inc., 31 East 2nd Street, Mineola, N.Y. 11501

Enlargement Guide

Sidelights—you know what they are; they are those little windows next to doorways, usually found in a home's entryway. Sidelights vary in size. So do your needs. Some individuals want sidelights to cover the entire opening while others simply desire to hang something "in front." We've given you a variety of different sizes to choose from. Often, we have found that 8" x 32" is a good size to sell at craft fairs, but you'll have to discover what your market requires and build accordingly.

Start by drawing the size of sidelight you wish to end up with onto a large sheet of paper. I have found the easiest way to enlarge the patterns in this book is to transfer them to a clear acetate sheet and then enlarge them onto your paper with an overhead projector. You can copy the pattern to the acetate in one of two ways. Have your local copy center do it for you (by having them use a copier to transfer it to a clear acetate sheet). Or, if you own a scanner, then scan the pattern into one of your computer programs and print it out on an appropriate 8½" x 11" clear acetate sheet. Then enlarge it on the overhead projector until it is the size you desire.

Of course, if you don't have an overhead projector (but do own a scanner, computer, and printer) you still have options. You can scan the pattern and then print it out on standard size paper. You'll just have to tape the different sheets of paper together to achieve the appropriate size.

Other options? Some copy centers have copiers that can make very large copies. So you could photocopy the pattern to the exact size you require with just the push of a button.

Helpful Hints

Our goal is to provide you with the best designs in stained glass. A great design with wonderful color selection is like a melody with great lyrics. However, in fairness, color can also take a bad design and make it "appear" acceptable. We'd rather concentrate on great design and let you concentrate on making the art come alive with color.

You are the artist. You shouldn't be overly influenced by other people's color ideas. We have observed over the years that while other artists often choose colors for our designs that we may not have chosen, often they are delightfully successful. Some exceed what we saw in our minds when designing the piece! This is exactly why we give you a small shaded drawing of the design rather than color photos of each piece. We ultimately believe that the artist will make the piece sing without our preconceived notions of color selection. You are the one who will take our designs and make them exceptional!

So when you look at the black-and-white pattern and wonder where you should go, trust your instincts. Make several copies of the pattern and color them in until you arrive at something that pleases you. If you only have certain colors of glass on hand in your studio, find creative ways to organize those colors. Experiment! The important thing is to make the best stained glass window you possibly can!

We have provided a shaded drawing alongside of the line drawing to help you define the focus of the pattern.

For a better quality stained glass window, approach stained glass as you would a fine painting. Think of where the light source would be in the scene. Consider this when you choose the stained glass and vary the shading from light to dark within each color group. Use such techniques as "atmospheric perspective" (darker, richer colors in the foreground and lighter, softer colors in the background) to achieve a feeling of distance. These techniques, combined with others you have learned will take your stained glass to the highest level possible.

Technical Hints

We use a strong ½" zinc border for all of our sidelights. This provides rigidity. We miter the corners and file any sharp edges. If it's a hanging piece (rather than one that fits into an opening), we solder loops on the top right and left corners. We also use strong jack chain because of the weight of the piece. The end-customer can easily hang the sidelight by inserting two hooks into their existing woodwork.

Other Hints

✦ Use mouth-blown rondels and glass nuggets in patterns that suggest these. Vary the shapes and colors for visual impact. Agates also make exceptional statements.

✦ Don't try to cut out small areas, such as a bird's eye, in stained glass. Instead, use a nice bead of rounded solder.

✦ Most of our customers have sidelights in their entryways. They want lots of light, but also privacy. Try to use a great deal of different clear textures and accent these with saturated cathedrals.

✦ For nature subjects, field guides offer a wealth of realistic color suggestions.

✦ Many of the designs invite wild color exploration (and a great way to use up your small scraps). Try using color variations you've never tried before. It's too easy to get in a "color rut." Be bold! Have fun!

Lotuses

Irises

Daisies and Fence 3

4   Daffodils

Morning Glories

You can make thorns out of slices of copper foil. Just burnish each thorn next to a lead line and then tin with solder. Easy thorns in no time!

Fuchsias

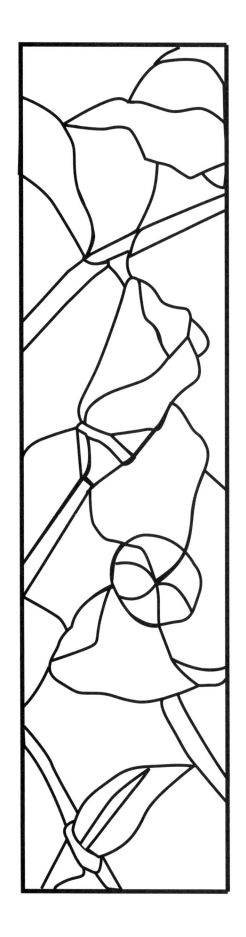
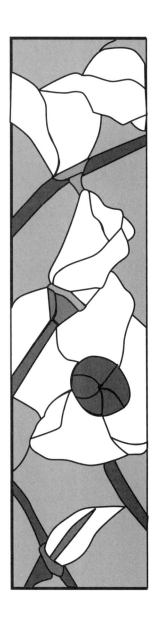

Poppies

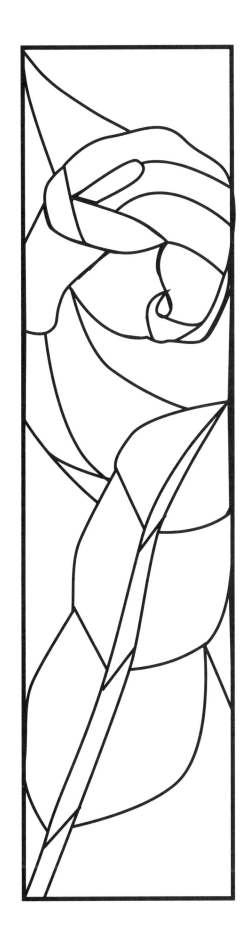
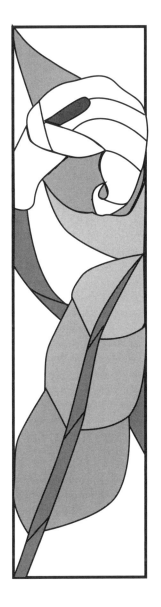

Calla Lilies

More Spring Daffodils

You can make thorns out of slices of copper foil. Just burnish each thorn next to a lead line and then tin with solder. Easy thorns in no time!

Iris Revisited

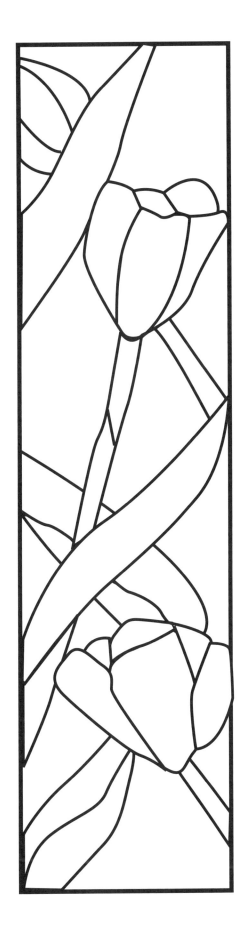
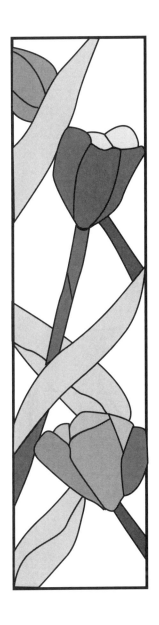

Tulip Dance

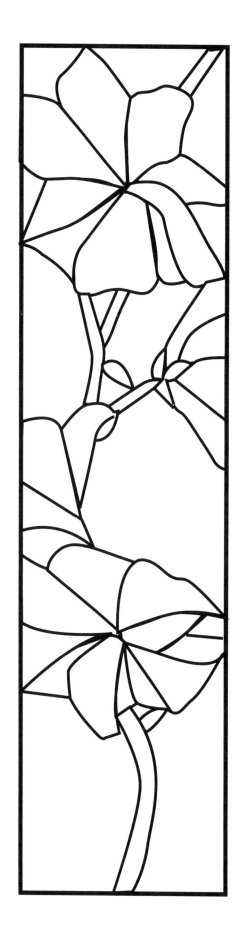
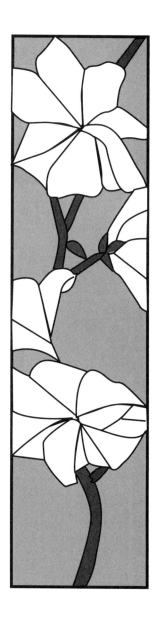

Stylized Petunias

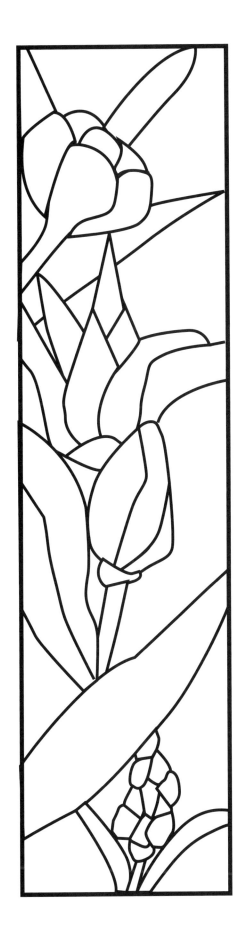
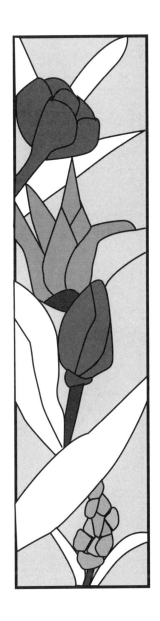

Crocus, Tulip, and Hyacinth

Pansies

Water Lilies

The stamens are copper wire bent into shape and attached at the lead lines.

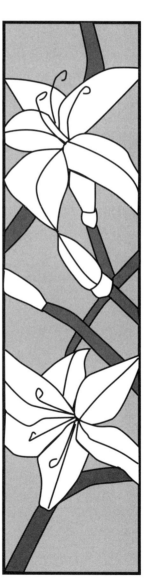

Day Lilies

Stylized Mums

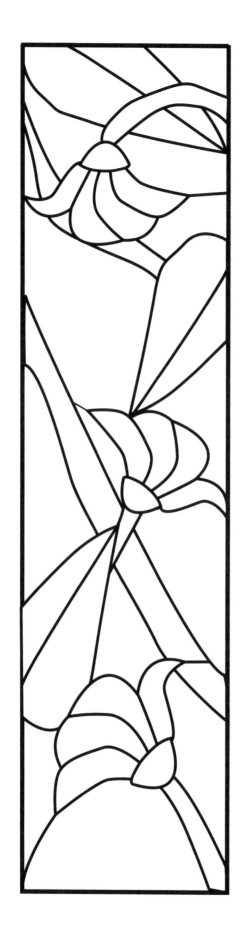

A Spring Day

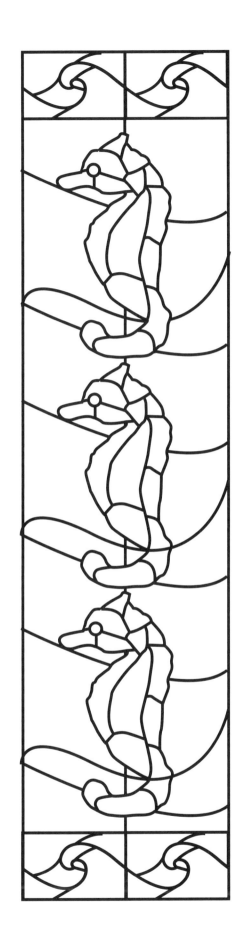

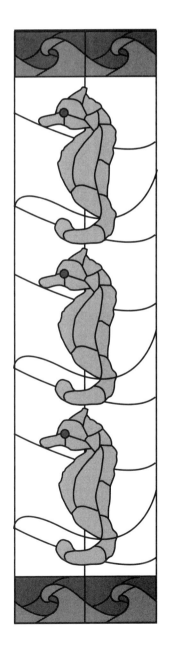

Seahorses

Blue Jay

Coyote

Sunflower

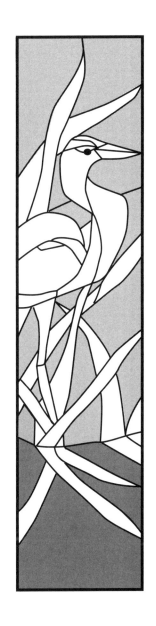

Great Blue Heron

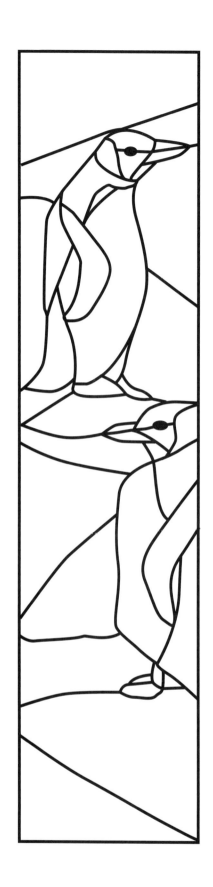
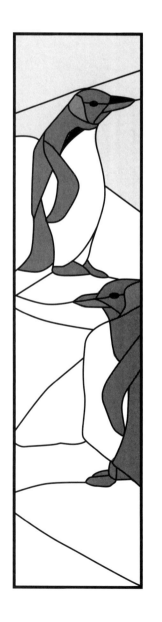

Penguins

Vine

Roadrunner and Quail

Flamingo

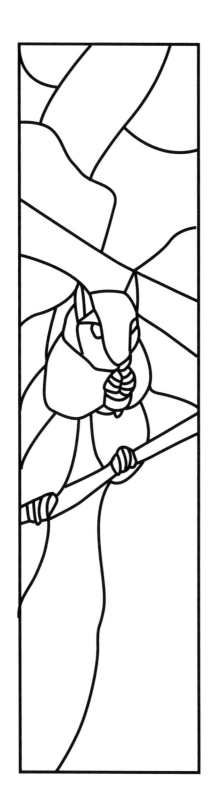

Squirrel

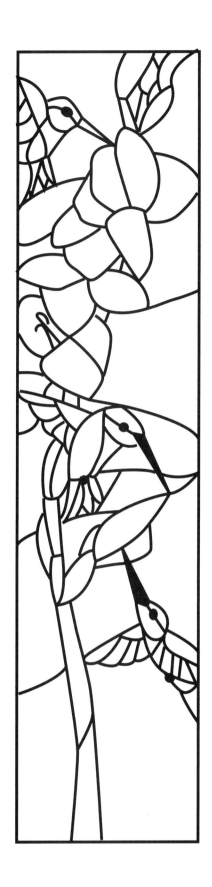

Hummingbirds

Dolphins

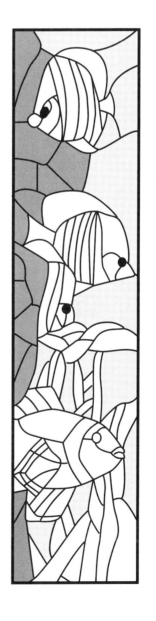

Fish

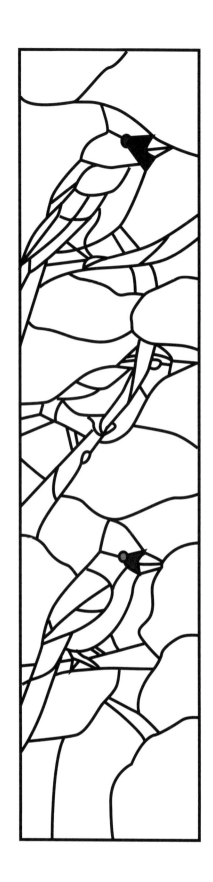

Cardinals and Nuthatch

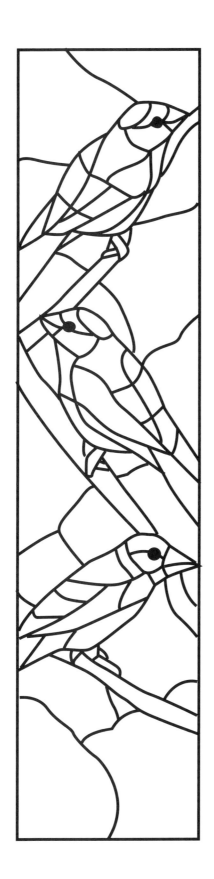
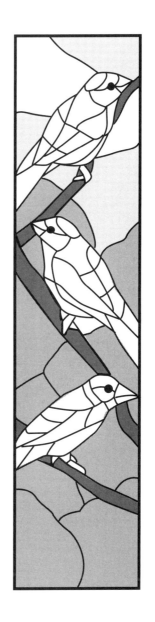

Evening Grosbeaks

Frog Pond

Chickadee and Pussy Willows

Pileated Woodpeckers

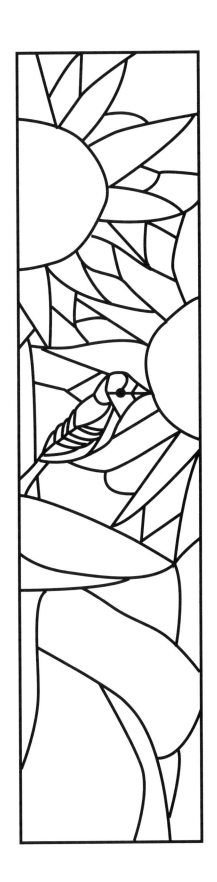
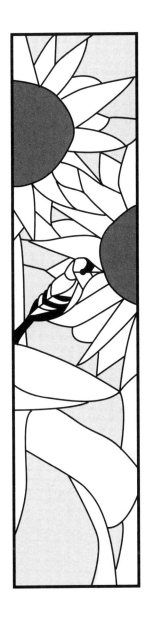

Sunflowers and Goldfinch

Cross and Lilies

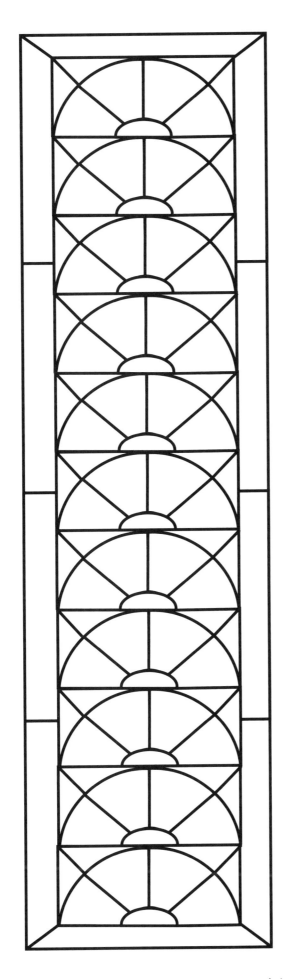
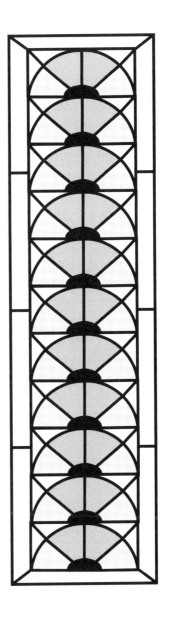

Fan . . . tastic!

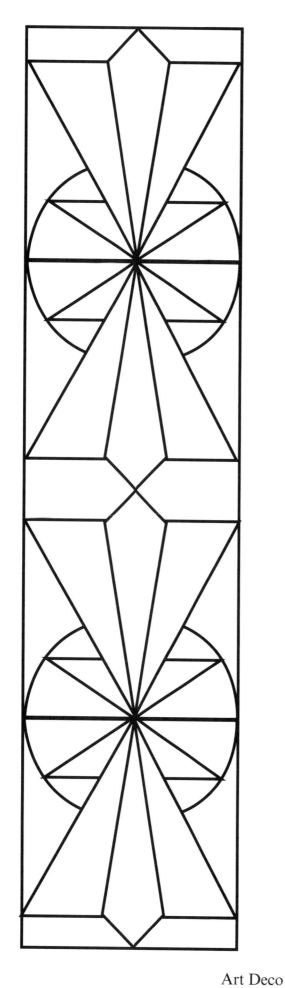
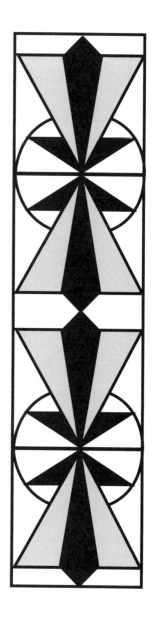

Art Deco

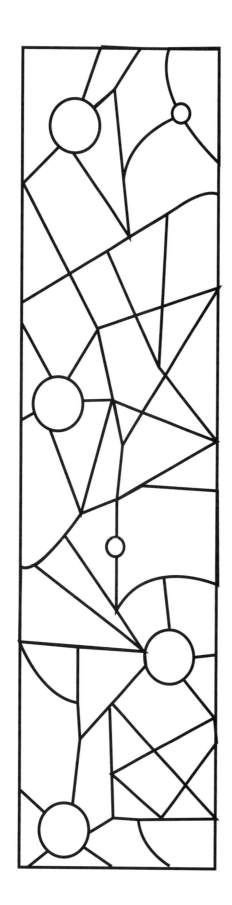

Abstract Dreams

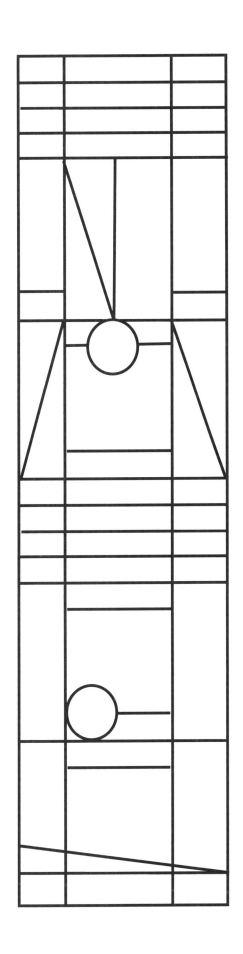
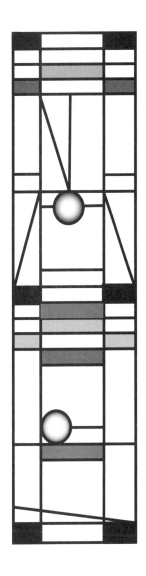

Moon Rest

Chains of Circles

Flying Geese

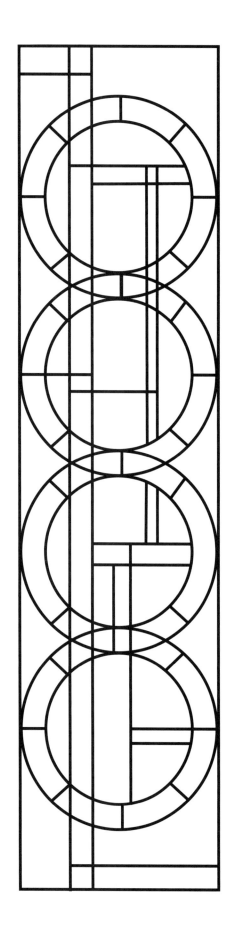
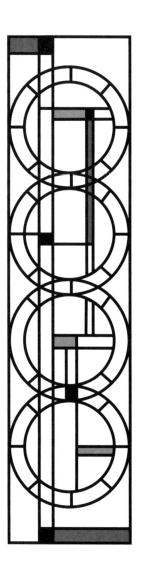

Commute

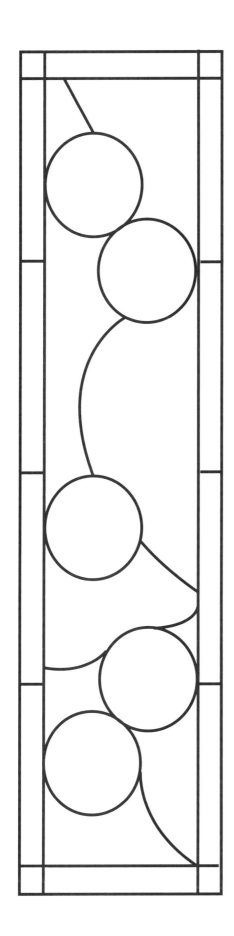
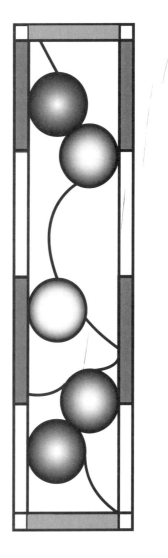

Cycles

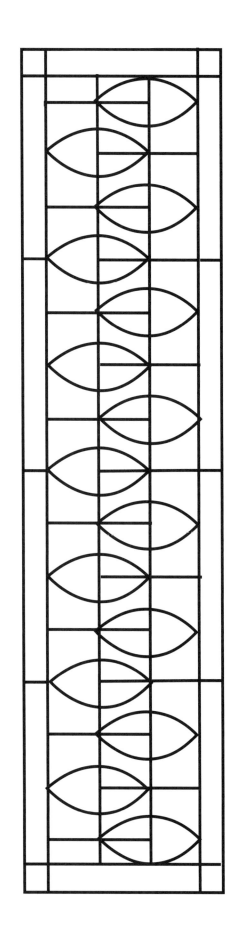

Leaves

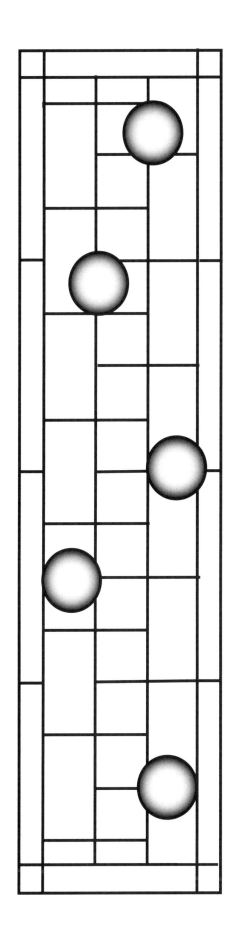

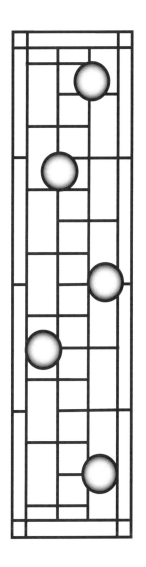

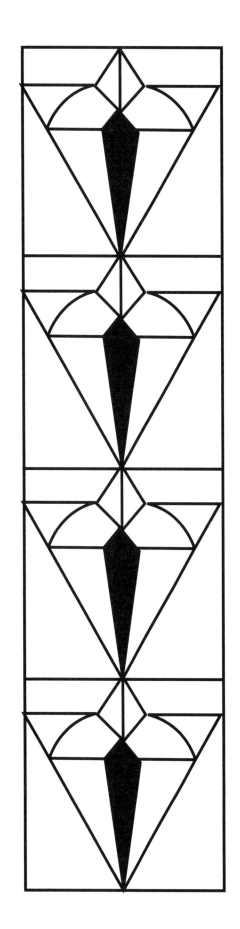

Deco Dance

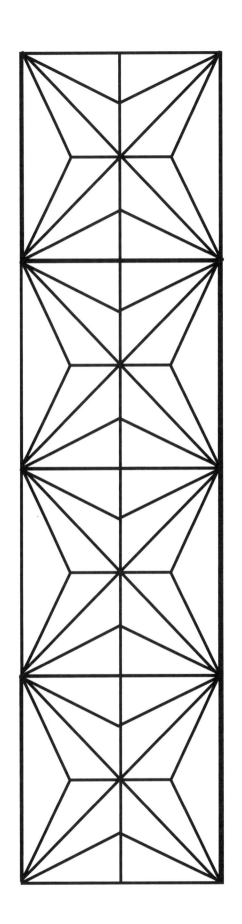

Celebration

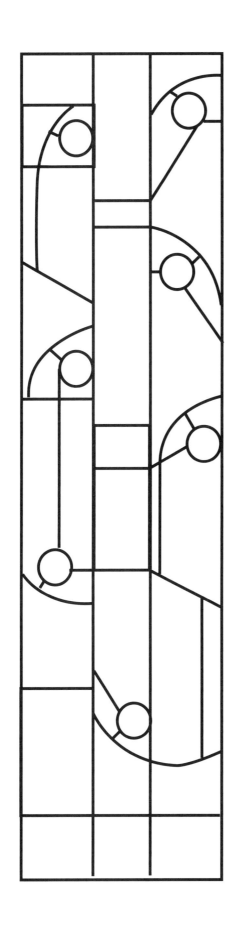
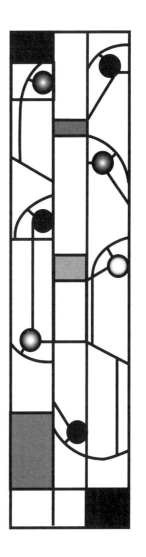

Motion

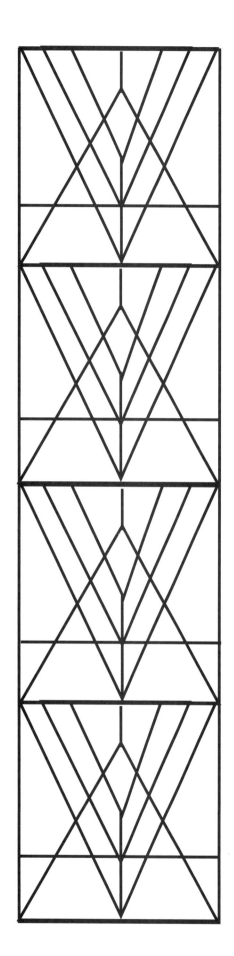

Mountains

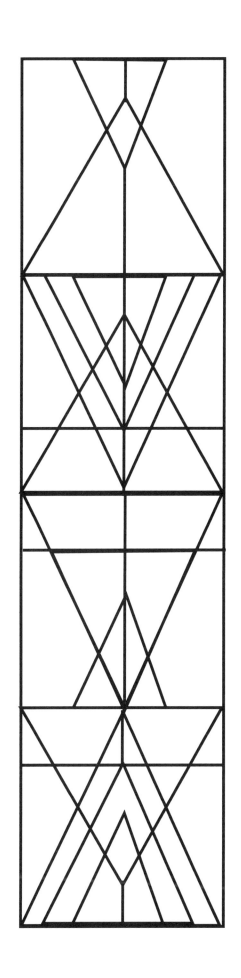

Torch

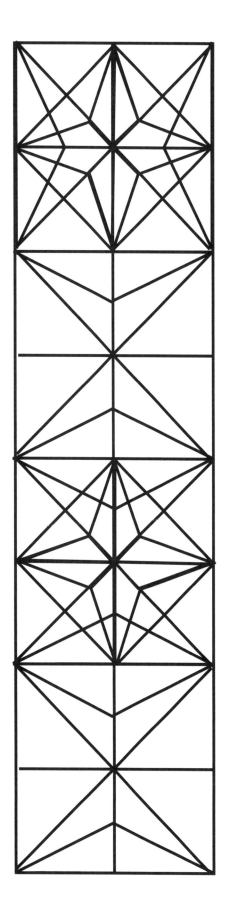

Try this in various clear textures!

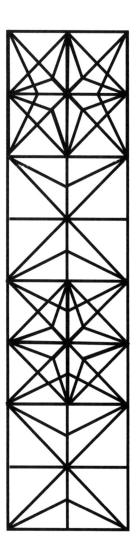

Changing

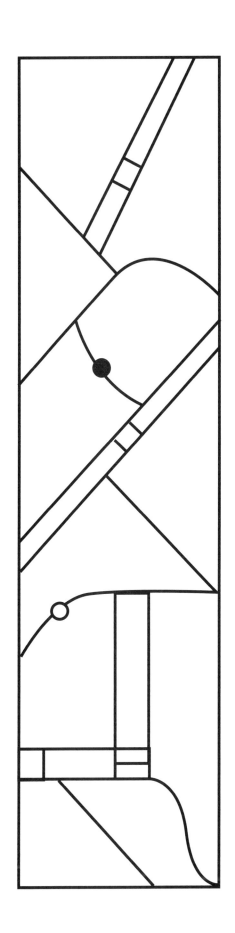

Complete in varying shades of blue. (Great for using up your smaller scraps!)

Ocean Escape